Museum of Things

poems by

Liz Chang

Finishing Line Press
Georgetown, Kentucky

Museum of Things

For my Calliope

Copyright © 2023 by Liz Chang
ISBN 978-1-64662-983-1 First Edition
All rights reserved under International and Pan-American Copyright Conventions. No part of this book may be reproduced in any manner whatsoever without written permission from the publisher, except in the case of brief quotations embodied in critical articles and reviews.

ACKNOWLEDGMENTS

The following poems appeared in *Exit 7: A Journal of Literature and Art*:

It's a Lamp, Charlie Brown
On Jolly Holiday
"She Couldn't Quite Explain It/[It] Had Always Just Been There…"

Publisher: Leah Huete de Maines
Editor: Christen Kincaid
Cover Art: "Whistler—the Peacock Room" by Xuan Che is licensed under CC-BY 2.0
Author Photo: Adrianne Mathiowetz Photography
Cover Design: Elizabeth Maines McCleavy

Order online: www.finishinglinepress.com
    also available on amazon.com

Author inquiries and mail orders:
Finishing Line Press
PO Box 1626
Georgetown, Kentucky 40324
USA

Table of Contents

It's a Lamp, Charlie Brown 1

"Truly, Truly, Truly Outrageous…!" 3

The Gift of Horseradish 5

Antoinette Who Called Herself 'Toni' 6

"Still Good" Rice Cooker, c. 1978 8

"She Couldn't Quite Explain It/
  [It] Had Always Just Been There…" 9

The Perfect Bathing Suit: A Forgery 11

Baby Gift, 1952 (?) 13

The Time Has Come, the Goddess Said,
  To Talk of Many Things (Assemblage #1) 15

On Jolly Holiday 19

Un-sippy Cup 21

The Moon and the Son (Assemblage #2) 23

Charles Schulz, 1922-2000
It's a Lamp, Charlie Brown
Ceramic Snoopy lampbase with plastic nightlight balloons (two missing, strings cut), topped with ivory paper lampshade printed with pictures of Peanuts characters flying kites
Snoopy base 5" tall, 17 ¼" to top of lampshade
Second Generation Chang family collection
1984.26

i.
My father says my mother says
we bought it from a store a few doors down
from his first office job. I always wondered
if it came from my grandparents, who sent
Schulz crib sheets from Hawaii,
paying whatever astronomical price to ship
printed cotton so many miles
as a declaration of their wishes for me,
that I might always be
uncomplicated, docile, faithful.

ii.
When I arrived, I was none of those things,
but I don't remember snubbing Snoopy
or his ceramic sidekick as I grew. I do remember
gazing at the balloons that never rose
while my mother recounted how my classmate
in the hospital might die from third degree burns
and how I cried and wished aloud that it could
have been me instead, feeling grief
flow out of me and into
the balloons' empty chambers.

iii.
In seventh grade, Snoopy toppled
from my high boy dresser, shattering
two of those balloons that had stayed
illuminated for so much of my childhood.
I recall the sound—a sternum cracking.
My father claims he bumped the lamp
one night while we were "disagreeing,"
but what echoes inside my head
my fault, my fault, my fault
belies this: all I can remember now
is picking up the shards, fallen
like so many scattered eggshells.

Hasboro, Inc.
"Truly, Truly, Truly Outrageous!..."
Three stickers from the Diamond JEM Sticker Collector's Album
(Nos. 89, 138 and 191), depicting stills from the animated
television series
2" tall x 2 ½" wide
Fourth generation Foster Collection
1986.51-53

My mother places them inside plastic eggs
for my little girls but before they can peel them
from their sticky backs, I confiscate them.
These are not precious: just colored ink

on paper old enough to contain something dangerous
as lead. But it is the story I am after,
the proof he loved me. With my girls and the eggs,
my mother tells me for the first time how

my grandfather (her father who sent
her possessions COD on the day of
her marriage to mine,
her father who did not know

my dad when he called
to say my mother had
had a baby, me) sent these stickers
to me for years after learning

that I sometimes watched the show.
I imagine I was many years past
enjoying the syrupy storylines
of a girl, who was secretly a Rockstar,

courtesy of her dead father
who'd programmed a computer
to transform her anytime she wanted,
with the touch of a magic earring.

Did he wish to transform me, transform us?
Were these stickers apology
for having passed judgment
on my existence before I even knew it?

Or were these the efforts
of a former philatelist who wished to pass along
something of his loss to me, after his younger son
stole his stamps to feed a habit?

I wish to forgive the way he drove
his golden child, his daughter,
to the opposite coast as she tried to move out of
the shadow Bob Foster cast from space.

He who could have built a magic
Rockstar-generating computer with spare parts,
a clean room, government funding,
and enough time.

I want to think the stickers letterless missives
mailed to a granddaughter he sought to understand
too late in life. Now the man I chose to share my life with
is most like him and we have daughters.

Most days I wish they could have met.
If my grandfather were to love him
and he loves me, it might
at last be a balanced equation.

Artist Unknown, b. mid-20th century
The Gift of Horseradish
Poured glass bottle, embossed Pierre Smirnoff label in red, white and gold
approx. 8" tall, 375ml capacity
Gift from the Ludmilla Foster collection
1986.56

Maybe she was out of practice
giving gifts, but I cannot imagine
what moved my mother's Russian aunt
to bring my temperate parents horseradish vodka
except to share a piece of her irrecoverable self.
It outlived her presence in their house.

                        My father so tired
of the balks of visiting vodka drinkers
he scrawled "horseradish" three times in Sharpie
on the embossed label in his neat hand.
On my mother in-law's first visit
to my parents' home, she ran her fingers
across the label's marred face and whispered, "what a shame—
that's a collector's item," and I didn't know
if I was meant to hear her.

Artist Unknown, b. early 20th century
Antoinette Who Called Herself 'Toni'
100% cotton peach towel with decorative flatwoven stripe,
personalized with script "AHF," embroidered in sienna thread
27 ½" x 15"
Third Generation Foster Collection
1996.66

I took it. A mail order department store
Royal Velvet hand towel from my grandmother's house
after she was gone. It is almost the ugliest color combination
I can imagine—its peachy pink fuzz promising perfection,
stained with nicotine-brown letters curling
like wisps of smoke.
It made my suitcase stink.

My great-grandmother Elizabeth got a Master's degree
in Art History, but her daughter—my Granny Toni—
tacked threadbare sheets on the windows as drapes
in her children's rooms. I hear this story from my mother's mouth
as evidence of my grandmother's Most Disappointing Quality.
But I recall her as raucous as Lucille Ball
and smooth as Elizabeth Taylor

in *National Velvet*, that for so long I mis-remembered
the brand of her towel. I look to this woman
who crisscrossed the country for love, walked away
from her chance to scratch her own mark on the century
as The Storytime Lady on Howdy Doody
or an executive for the NEA, choosing instead
to follow Bob as he blazed a vapor trail across the continent.

But sometimes flecks of only her bleed through.
Her 1962 cover letter closes, "There is no doubt but
what I am far easier to live with
when I am happy and fulfilled."
She knew all the secrets of having a family and vocation
long before I try—how to unseal a stuck lid
without asking a man (bang it upside-down on the ground

like you're calling the downstairs neighbor),
how to boil eggs so the yolks stay yellow
(boil them up then all the way down),
take every minute they give you.
She'd say it's all about finesse,
but I've heard tell of her teaching whole days
wearing one black shoe and one blue.

And so, a hand towel bares our worst—
smeared slime of digits rinsed hastily, bits picked
from teeth or nose. She'd laugh to hear I pinched it.
She might smile to know that when
my mother wants to compliment me
she'll say I look like her mother
or that I laugh

like her mother or that
she sometimes thinks
her mother has sent her
handwritten notes from the Beyond
when she gets mail from me.
Turns out,
I have her hand.

Artist Unknown, b. early 20th century
"Still Good" Rice Cooker, c. 1978
glazed avocado green steel with nested electronics, black handles,
replaced wooden top
10" x 9" x 7 ½", 6-cup capacity
Second Generation Chang Family collection
2001.05

It might have had a name, an older sibling when I was growing up,
its pale green body and haughty flick of beetle's wings closing
to announce another successfully completed job
that I hear three rooms away.

With the handle my father carefully replaced at least twice
—chanting "still good" under his breath—it plods
along making rice that never burns
but forms a bubbled, cracked skin each time on the inside lip
where the belly meets the lid.
When I was small, I remember impatiently waiting
for the metal to cool and peeling away
the starched shed skin in strips.
The crack and rustle so satisfying.

My father passed it to me when I left his home for college.
I swear he would've buckled it into a seatbelt
if I hadn't been watching.

Liz Chang, b. 1983
**"She Couldn't Quite Explain It/
[It] Had Always Just Been There..."**
Wooden display shelf, four shelves total; painted white with shelf
paper (library print) with two metal rings on outside face
29" x 9" x 5 ¾"
Anonymous donation
2005.13

Wednesday mornings in the West Village
trash trucks lumber up the narrow streets early enough
to sound like rebuke, their metal bodies screech
and seize, startle us from slumber.
No residents stir that early—only shopworkers
blasting vomit from front stoops, scraping dogshit from the curb.

We took to scouring the sidewalks on springtime Tuesday evenings,
picking through the well-off's cast-offs, their casual
disregard, rather than face our own crumbling.
Or maybe it was just me who found solace not meeting
his eyes but walking beside him, not holding his hand,
searching other people's garbage for redemption.

When I pulled the mint green shelf from its grave
wedged between tightly tied trash bags, he scoffed
and held his nose at the smell, pointed out the large chunk
of wood knocked from the front face.
I felt the weight of its past
like a stray kitten in my arms.

Everything permanent he'd let me bring
into our space was earthtoned—it was defiantly wrong,
too loud and odd like me. I hung it by the door,
its prominence reminding us both
of our coming dissolution, as if
we had circled it on our internal calendars.

Later we walked the same streets to brunch,
the pavement mostly clear of the week's refuse.
He stopped near a sidewalked bin to flip through CDs
gasped to find the Crash Test Dummies'
God Shuffled His Feet among the discards.
In five years together, he had never mentioned

even liking the band, but I saw the old love I missed
igniting in his eyes, and he surprised us both
by deciding to buy it for me.
I accepted his token mournfully, thinking
this is a gift you give your middle school carpool lead
or a lab partner—not someone who's carried and lost your child.

I began listening to it out of obligation, found even
fewer words to explain my sorrow. But when
he was out late nights working, I retreated
under my comforter as the lead singer hummed the unsayable:
Mmmm mmm mmmm mmm, carefully placed it back
on my shelf before he returned.

I lost that CD long ago, but I've carried
this hideous shelf through five moves,
a marriage and children. Last year I whitewashed it,
added excess wallpaper to each surface,
trying to fit it into my new life.
It hangs in the only room that's mine.

Artist Unknown
The Perfect Bathing Suit: A Forgery
Ivory one-piece bandeau-style bathing suit with front center
ruching beginning at bodice, "Delfina" tag, size Large;
80% Nylon, 20% Lycra
14" wide at chest, 11 ½" at waist and 20" long [measured flat]
Provenance Unknown
2006.02

I found my perfect suit when I was in college:
a marble white one-piece with a ruched neckline
and legs cut to hug my curves just right.

A Marilyn-Monroe number, but not
sad Marilyn, naked and bloated
as a discarded fish on the deck of a boat—

early Norma Jean. I believed myself transformed
inside the white suit, white shell.
So un-Marilyn in my darkness,

maybe I imagined my bathing body on retro
travel posters for Hawaii, my father's home state.
But even that, a lie. My family

of import/export children
from a grocery store line.
I wore this perfect suit once

to a TV-famous actor's beach house,
willed myself to belong, committed to feeling
at home on a sunwashed lounger.

At the end of the day in his swanky
powder room, I peeled away my Hollywood,
avoided the full-length mirror looking back.

This must be how beautiful people live:
an opportunity to gaze at perfection
in every room. Illusion crushed,

I stuffed the perfect suit
into the very bottom of my bag.
When I got home, just empty space.

Years later I pull a pearly exoskeleton from the corner
of a "last look before donation" box.
The aged nylon crunches in my hands,

elastic of each leghole creaking
like crepidation. I think back
to the summer in my childhood

when I found perfectly perched cicada skins
still clinging valiantly under the white-flower
shade of our dogwood tree,

how I crushed them between curiously forlorn
fingertips. It is hard to believe
that a warm, living thing

once smoothly filled
this architecture.
That she is gone.

Artist Unknown, 1927-2019 or 1929-2013
Baby Gift, 1952 (?)
Cardboard shirt box with white acrylic baby sweater inside
14 ¼" x 9 ½" x 2", baby sweater sized 6-12 months
Third Generation Chang Family Collection
2007.679

Before my father and I moved my grandmother
from her tropical rental in Hawaii into my parents' basement

on the frigid Eastern seaboard, she pulled
treasures out of the top of her closet

and showed each to me conspiratorially.
This was before I was married.

Like an aging magician, she revealed a tone-on-tone
printed cardboard box from Clothier's

with the label *Baby Gift* in either her
or my grandfather's writing.

(I never could tell them apart—
the mark of a marriage so long gone.)

She carefully removed the white knit sweater
to show off how delicate it was,

folding it back into its home
and patting it with satisfaction

the way a pregnant mother
pats her belly—as if the box contained an actual baby.

I couldn't tell if it had been given to her
when my father was young

or if she still intended to gift it
or if she had made it or bought it

or commissioned it. I didn't ask—
she was no longer anchored to this world. Years later,

when my daughter was born,
my mother excavated the box.

She had not been there
to see the pride on my grandmother's face,

so she tossed it at me with a
"here, you might as well use this."

But I never dressed my daughter in white
and now it lives

on her highest closet shelf,
perched like a knowing ghost.

Assemblage: Two Objects
**The Time Has Come, the Goddess said,
To Talk of Many Things**

Artist Unknown, b. early twentieth century
Cast porcelain statue of goddess Guanyin, standing on a lotus
blossom with an orange or globe of light in her left hand; crack at
neck repaired with epoxy, missing three fingers from her right hand
12" from base to top of figure (figure 10.5" tall), base 4 ¼" across
Third generation Chang family collection
2007.136

Artist Unknown, b. mid-twentieth century
Crabtree and Evelyn cast Walrus in waistcoat and bowtie in
rosemary-scented castile soap from the Alice in Wonderland
collection, 1980
3 ¾" tall, 2" wide base (splayed feet)
Second generation Chang family collection
2010.102

i.
Milk-white and serene, the goddess surveys my bedroom.
Her eyes are pinprick concavities punched into her head

under heavy lids. In middle school when I first try
to apply drugstore make-up, I learn I have these same

eyelids, that lack of Cover Girl crease. I have read
that Guanyin hears the cries of the world but

her lobes are pendulous, earholes bored into the cast.
I cannot see the bottom. She must hear the news each morning

as I do, but she does not flinch. Does she hear
the blustering last president christen this unyielding virus

"Kung Flu"? Does she hear my pain and surprise when
the sheriff claims the shooter was *having a bad day*

as he swept six women with families
from this earth? She must have heard me cry

on my husband's chest that night, afraid to walk outside
alone or with my daughters. The goddess stands

silently by. Before she was mine, she lost her head—
maybe that's when her waters of compassion leaked out.

ii.
The walrus was a gift to my parents
on their interracial wedding day from their ringbearer.

His namesake versed in cabbages and kings but
he is a child's gift, this cast fancy soap.

When I find the box shoved to the back of their closet
with his nephew's note still attached, my father

does not pause to answer my questions.
Everything about him says *withdraw*.

The walrus tucks his flippers toward nonexistent pockets.
His tusks brush the lapels on his vest.

I found this soap twenty years after it was given
as if it had been hidden there next to shame. He looks up

to the sky beyond articulated whiskers
through beady eyes with a look to wash away the world.

I have lived a life that means I believe this:
darkened eyes connote dishonesty. I have dark eyes.

iii.
Before she was mine, Guanyin's head was off'd
then glued back on. I imagine an accident while

someone tidied my grandmother's bedroom,
or maybe it was something more sinister—

an angry regent of whiteness. Maybe the red queen
or someone who wished to suck out the power of a wise

old woman grieving for the world. Only young
women are supposed to speak. (And they can only purr.)

On the news: old women pushed to the ground,
punished for existing. We are crazy for complaining—

we are the Model Minority, right? We have it easy and
can we even trust what we see with our own crooked eyes?

iv.
The walrus is unsteady in first position, weighed down
by his gentleman's scarf. He pitches forward regularly,

bears the scars to prove it. I never knew my mother
to enjoy Lewis Carroll, but perhaps the ringbearer,

her soon-to-be-nephew knew what she did not:
that unmoored feeling of a lone white face floating

in the sea of Asian tradition. The fall through
the looking-glass and out the other side of the world.

I see wedding pictures of my blond mother draped in a tea leaf lei
conspicuously missing the parents-of-the-bride.

When I am older, she tries to explain that she never expected
to love a Chinese man, but she found she loved

all of the things he was because he was Chinese.
She worries aloud what this would do

to her children. She does not hear this last part land on me,
see it capsize me.

v.
Between these two poles, I make a home.

Anonymous
On Jolly Holiday
Pink parasol-style 100% Nylon umbrella with ruffles, one painted
unicorn and four "Elizabeth"s in grey, curling script, hooked
plastic handle, steel shaft and ribs
24" thrust, 34" diameter span
Second Generation Chang Family collection
1989.80

While traveling, my father's heart softened
to the call of an elderly street vendor,
Asian and stooped, quiet until he saw us
moving toward him on the sidewalk.
Until that moment, I'd been young enough
to scramble under my mother's wing,
sheltered by her shared teal umbrella.
Now choosing my own feels so grown-up.

The man plucks it silently from his wire cart
and pushes it open, twirling its petals round
and round. I remember the shape of his gnarled hand,
finger reaching outward like a slack mouth,
as he personalized it with marker pen, replicating
the exact flourish of *z* and *h* each time
he reached a new panel. I stood there long enough
to be embarrassed, while he finished the job
with red hearts to hide one tiny smudge,
for which he mimed apology, all of it
an elaborate choreograph for my benefit.

When at last I pushed it open and it stuck,
I hoped the world under my feet would shift
like Mary Poppins' chalk-drawn world,
and I would be transported into a dream—
where—instead of the clumsy waiter-penguin I'd played
in the camp show, when four younger penguins
berated me for not remembering the dance,

pulling tears from my eyes
that surprised even me—
I could emerge as beautiful Jane Banks
with her coifed hair and rosy cheeks,
her broad blue eyes.

I never stopped imagining myself
reborn. When my first daughter came,
she surprised us all by shedding
her dark hair-tufts in her fourth month.
Her hair grew back in blond.
I see her rosy-cheeked and round as
young Miss Banks, and I was foolish enough
to believe that this world
might be easier on her. I watch her
rummage that pink umbrella
from my parents' house, stroll under it
in the Sunday sun with it as shield.

One day after dance class, she cries
that the other girls won't be friends
with her because of her skin.
I want to scream and slash the air,
but instead, I say that her skin
marks her as part of our family,
that one day those girls will envy
her perfect tan. I am not sure
she accepts this explanation.
But we both put down the weight of it
and walk into the chalk-line sunset.

Artist Unknown, b. 20th century
The Un-Sippy Cup
frosted plastic, child-sized beer stein with 'Merion School'
printed in red block letters
5 ½" x 2 ½" diameter with 1½" handhold span (½" to thumb
impression)
Second Generation Chang Family collection
2020.479

Now my daughter drinks from the cup,
the one I won as a door prize at the fair
in elementary school. The fair where we threw rings
around Coke bottle necks and sipped lemon juice
jammed into the flesh of citrus half-suns
through striped sugar straws, pretending
we hadn't been marked
as "no longer children"
just months before
when a plane fell from the sky,
the burnt-out husk
of a helicopter coiled around it
like a flaming nest
and the jet fuel watered our hand-clipped
baseball field so that it smelled
like heady death for weeks while we traded
stickers in scorched ditches,
shallow graves.

When I won this cup,
I did not blink at its foreign bulk
its adult curves and double bottom,
but now I wonder whose catalogue ordering pre-
internet made all of us eight year-olds
imitation *biergarten* Juicy Juice sloshers.
Even the sans serif red letters aged us,

standing at attention as clear and crisp
as any college logo, leaving off
the tag of what should have been
…Elementary, my darling. But this is
where and when I grew up.

I watch my oldest drink in childhood
and I wonder how it will happen for her.
She is losing teeth. As the new ones
thrust up from inside her watermelon pink gums,
I realize I do not know
how to lead her through the extinguishing light
of childhood—for me
it happened all at once.
But I swear I would hollow myself
around her as a shield
to shade her one more moment
so that she may drink her fill.

Assemblage: Two Objects
The Moon and the Son

Marilee Heyer
The Weaving of a Dream: a Retold Chinese Folktale children's book, Puffin Classics in 10pt cover gloss paper and 85lb text paper, perfect bound
10 ¾" x 8 ¼" x ¼"
Second Generation Chang Family collection
1989.38

Michael Chang, b. 1952
white plastic globe around LED bulb with black base from old lamppost, balanced on hollowed out wooden bowl, electronics (corded switch)
14" from base to top, 10 ½" globe diameter, 5" base diameter
Second Generation Chang Family collection
2014.78

My father read to me from his passed down library
of Golden Books—books for little American children—
and I learned that stories weren't about people who looked
like us. I felt my Asian-ness a secret, one
that the authors did not know or understand.

But once I found *The Weaving of a Dream*
tucked in among the many golden spines,
a retold Chinese fairy tale of three sons—no daughters—
about a parent who asks the impossible after
falling in love with art, the wind snatching away her happiness.

Of course, it is the youngest son who stays the longest,
remains loyal and courageous. My father is the youngest,
and when his mother faltered, he did not hesitate
to knock out his front teeth, swallow his cries
as he flew over fire, stifle screams as he lolled in a vast sea of grief.

Reading this book, I remember tracing the confident curl
of the handdrawn cat with the pad of my finger
as it rested at the mother's bedside, how its back intertwined
in my mind with the line about the parent
who loves the one perfect child the best.

And though the story does not mention the cat,
I knew this to be true.

At the end of his journey, the youngest son
at last traces his mother's weaving
to a palace of fairies and monsters. At night,
the most beautiful fairy hangs a pearl to work by as a lamp.
It is elemental as the moon, this love of art and beauty.

When the old streetlamp snuffed out outside
my childhood home, my father brought me with him
to help him choose a new one. The one I liked
did not match the style of our modest home, but it shone
like the moon beyond our door.

Every night I imagined I could see the curve
of a fairy's cupped hands in the soft brown dark
that enfolded it. Before we sold that house,
my father took down the globe,
replaced it.

He fashioned a lamp base from a bottomless bowl,
rewired the moon so it would not glow too hot,
gifted it to me many years later so I can read
to my daughters at night
by its light.

He never says, we share these things, a history.
He does not say, you are mine.

Liz Chang was 2012 Montgomery County Poet Laureate in Pennsylvania. Her poems have appeared in *Verse Daily, Rock & Sling, Origins Journal, Breakwater Review* and *Stoneboat Literary Journal*, among others. Her translations of French poet Claude de Burine's work were published in *The Adirondack Review*. Her first two poetry collections (*Provenance* and *What Ordinary Objects*) are available from Book-Arts Press. Her other chapbook, *Animal Nocturne*, was published by Moonstone Press in 2018. Chang's creative nonfiction has recently appeared in *Oyster River Pages*, and her flash fiction was published internationally.

Liz is Visiting Assistant Professor of Creative Writing at Moravian University. She lives with her family, a dog, a cat, and a hive of honeybees *en les environs* of Philadelphia.

www.ingramcontent.com/pod-product-compliance
Lightning Source LLC
Chambersburg PA
CBHW022129090426
42743CB00008B/1063